How To Play
GUITAR

A Complete Guide
for Absolute Beginners

Ben Parker

Author: Ben Parker

Editor: Alison McNicol

First published in 2012 by Kyle Craig Publishing

This version updated Dec 2014

Text and illustration copyright © 2012 Kyle Craig Publishing

Design and illustration: Julie Anson

Music set by Ben Parker using Sibelius software

ISBN: 978 -1-908-707-09-3

A CIP record for this book is available from the British Library.

A Kyle Craig Publication
www.kyle-craig.com

Contents

Introduction

Welcome to **How To Play The Guitar**. The Guitar is probably the most popular instrument for beginners who wish to start playing a string instrument.

In this book we aim to give you your first simple steps to playing which can act as a basis for a bright future with the instrument. Also included in the book is a step by step guide to reading music.

Practice

Like any skill, playing an instrument takes a lot of practice. Practicing more regularly for shorter lengths of time is more effective than practicing for an hour or so just once a week. The minimum amount would be around 15-20 minutes, 3 to 4 times a week. The ideal amount would be 20 minutes a day, 7 days a week. Maybe set out a plan of your week and work out the best times to fit your practicing around the other things you do. The more your practice can become part of your weekly or daily routine the better.

Remember, little and often is best!

About The Guitar

The guitar originates from a group of European string instruments played in the 12th century. The guitar as we know it today began taking its current form in the 15th and 16th centuries when a Spanish instrument called a 'Vihuela' was developed. Like a medieval Lute, the Vihuela had six strings and a curved body.

The guitar comes in many types, shapes and sizes. The most popular types of guitar used today are **steel string acoustic guitars** and **electric guitars,** although beginners often begin by playing a nylon string (or Classical) guitar.

On the guitar you can play both **chords** and **single notes, strum** and **pick**. These different ways of playing make it an interesting instrument to learn, with different stages of ability as your skills progress.

The Instrument

ACOUSTIC

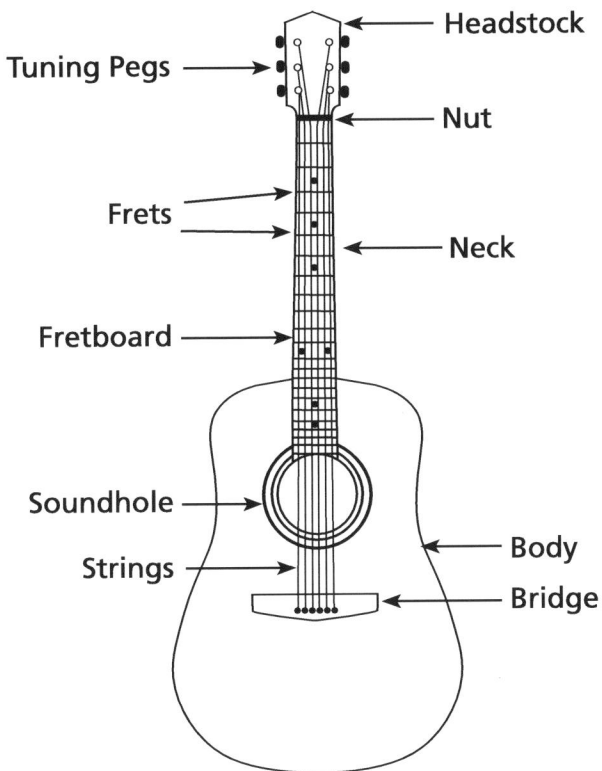

Tuning Pegs
Headstock
Nut
Frets
Neck
Fretboard
Soundhole
Strings
Body
Bridge

ELECTRIC

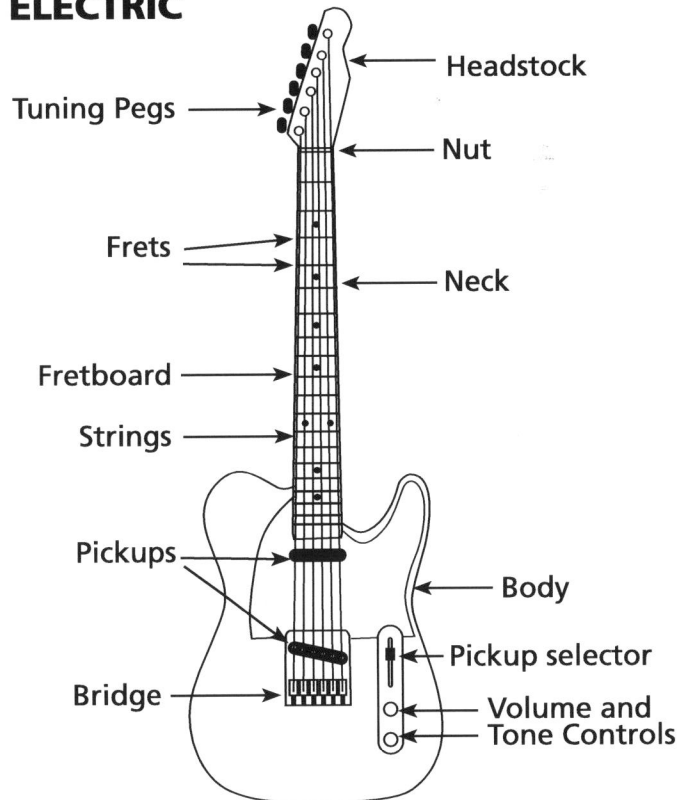

Tuning Pegs
Headstock
Nut
Frets
Neck
Fretboard
Strings
Pickups
Body
Bridge
Pickup selector
Volume and Tone Controls

How To Hold The Guitar

As a beginner you are likely to feel the most comfortable playing sitting down, with the curve of the guitar body resting on your right leg. Make sure you choose a seat or stool that allows your feet to sit flat on the floor. If you have a strap you can also try playing standing up.

What To Do With Your Hands

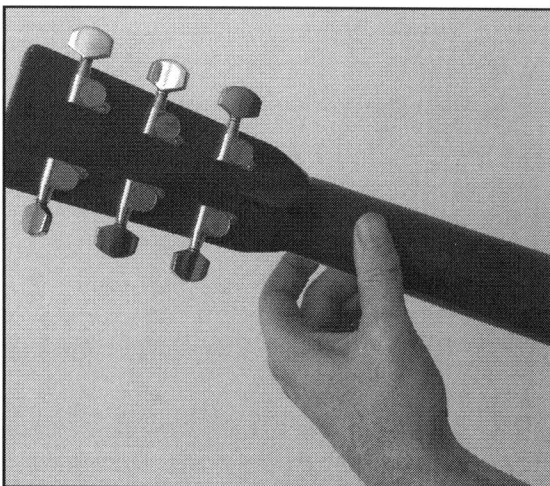

LEFT HAND POSITION

Your left hand position is really important. Make sure your thumb is around the back of the neck. When you fret a note it should be like 'pinching' the neck between your thumb and forefinger. Fretting will be explained in more detail later on in the book.

RIGHT HAND POSITION

Your right arm will naturally hang over the body of the guitar, dropping your right hand down to where the strings are. To begin with you should rest your thumb on the bottom (thickest) string and pull up on the strings to pluck them. Alternatively you can use a pick or plectrum.

LEFT HANDED PLAYERS

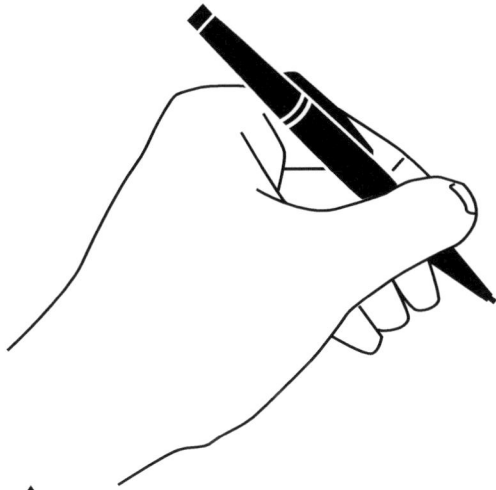

Some left handed players play the guitar right-handed. If you are left-handed try the playing position shown and see how it feels. If it feels strange, try playing it the other way round (with the guitar headstock pointing to your right) if this position feels more comfortable then you will need to have the guitar re-strung upside down. Ask at your local music store — they should be able to do this for you.

Using A Plectrum/Pick

You can use your right hand fingers to play the guitar but many players use a **plectrum** (often called a **pick**) to strum chords and pick single notes. It is best to strum across the soundhole of the guitar. If strumming with your fingers (without a pick) use your thumb to strum downwards and your fingers for the upstroke.

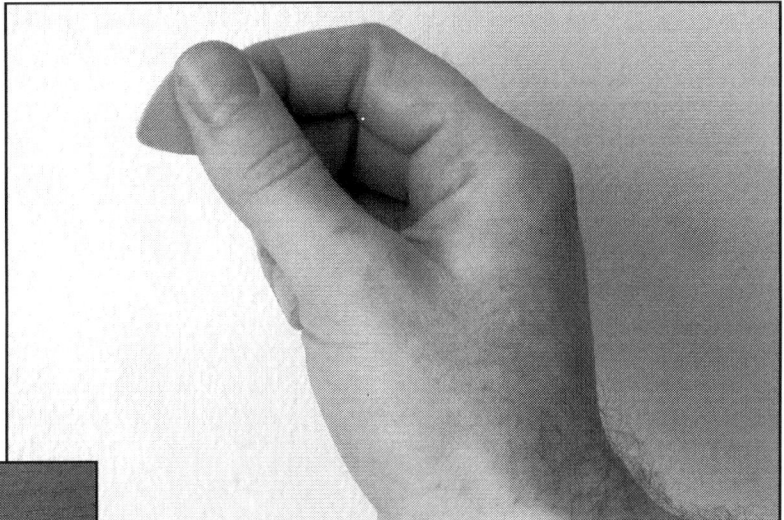

Picks come in different thicknesses. A pick of medium thickness (nylon .60mm) is probably the best place to start. A brighter tone can be produced with a pick and most players find it easier to move swiftly between playing chords and single notes when using one. There will also be more about picking the strings with your right hand fingers later on in the book.

Tuning

The strings of the guitar are tuned to the notes **E, A, D, G, B, E**. These strings are known as the **'open'** strings. Pressing down on a string with a left hand finger to change the pitch of the note is called fretting. The strings are also numbered to help us when referring to them.

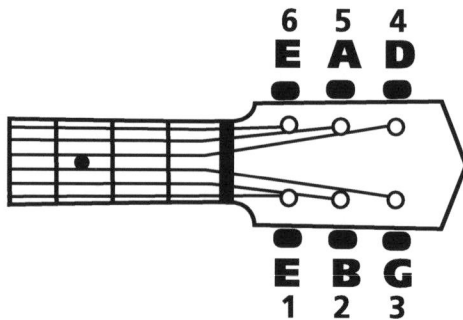

TUNING PEGS	To Make Your Note Lower	To Make Your Note Higher
TURN PEGS ON TOP ROW (E, A & D strings)	CLOCKWISE	ANTI-CLOCKWISE
TURN PEGS ON BOTTOM ROW (G, B & E strings)	ANTI-CLOCKWISE	CLOCKWISE

The Open Strings

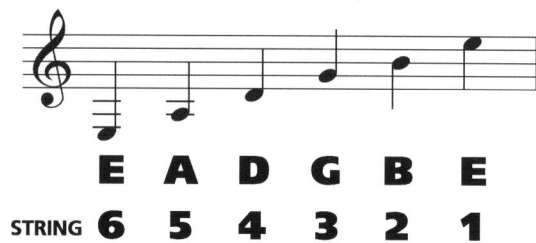

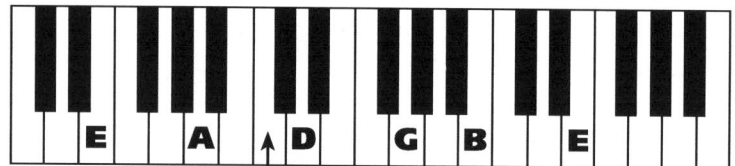

"Middle C" on piano

To keep your guitar in tune you can either use a pitched instrument such as the piano to give you reference pitches or you can use one of the many digital tuning apps now available for smartphones and laptops. There are also certain websites which give you a 'player' which allows you to play recorded guitar notes as a reference.

*PLEASE NOTE that the above guide is for acoustic steel string guitars and classical/nylon string guitars — your tuning method may have to change when tuning some electric guitars or other guitars with all the tuning pegs on one side of the headstock.

Strings And Things

Caring For Your Guitar

You can keep the body of your guitar clean using a polishing cloth and some (wooden) furniture polish. This should get rid of any smears or fingerprints from handling the guitar. You can also wipe the strings down too. Hold a clean cloth (not a polishing cloth) and 'pinch' the string between your thumb and index finger and run your 'pinched' fingers the whole length of the string. This should get rid of any grease that builds up from sweat etc. whilst playing.

Stretching The Strings

Sometimes, especially with new instruments, you may find that soon after you have tuned your guitar, it will quickly go out of tune again. This does not always mean you have a poor quality instrument, rather that you are experiencing string 'slippage'. Where the strings haven't had enough time to 'bed in' it may be difficult for them to stay in tune. When this occurs try stretching the strings by pulling each one individually away from the fretboard by about 3cm (be careful with this). This will probably take the string out of tune. Tune it back to its pitch and stretch again. Repeat this process until the string no longer drops in pitch when stretched.

Choosing Strings

Guitar strings come in different gauges. This is essentially how 'thick' the strings are. The sound and playability of your guitar will change according to the string gauge. *Higher* (or 'heavy') gauge strings have a greater tension, are louder but harder to press down when fretting. *Lower* (or 'light') gauge strings have less tension, are quieter but much easier to press down when fretting.

Average measurements
(thousandths of an inch)
for string gauges tend to look like this:

Electric Guitar Strings   .009 - .042
Acoustic Steel Strings   .012 - .052
Classical Nylon Strings .028 - .043

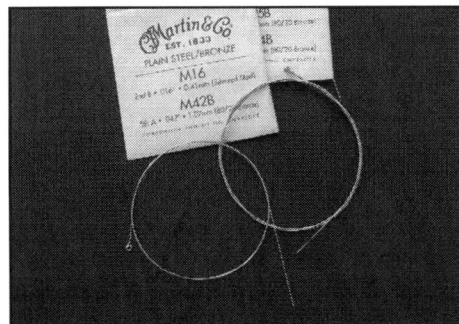

Knowing Your Notes

The notes on the music stave (see below) either sit on the lines or in the spaces. As notes go higher vertically on the stave they go higher in pitch. As they go lower vertically on the stave they go lower in pitch. To help us remember the notes in the spaces, think 'SPACE' rhymes with 'FACE'. To help us remember the notes on the lines, the first letters of each of the words 'Every Good Boy Deserves Football', make up the notes on the lines of the stave as they go UP.

Notes in the spaces

F A C E

Notes on the lines

E G B D F

Music runs alphabetically from **A** to **G** and then starts again on **A**. When notes go above or below the stave we use **ledger lines** to keep track of how many spaces/lines down or up they are.

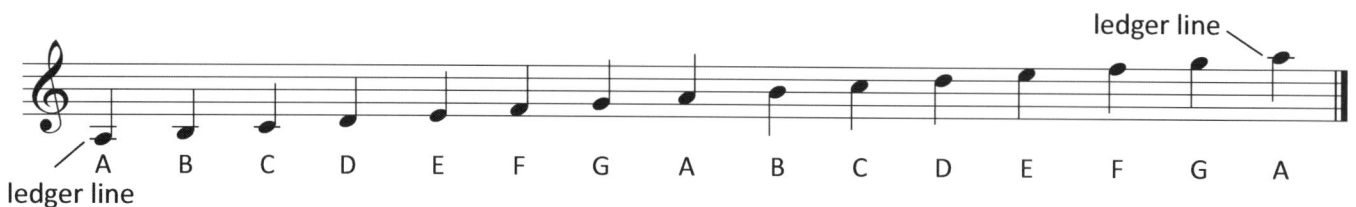

ledger line

A   B   C   D   E   F   G   A   B   C   D   E   F   G   A

ledger line

Your guitar's lowest note is the open **E** string (string 6) and the highest note of most acoustic guitars is a high **C** (way up on the 20th fret of the top **E** string!). This is what is called the **range** of the instrument.

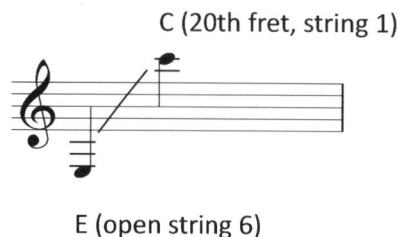

C (20th fret, string 1)

E (open string 6)

Other Musical Symbols

There are many symbols used in written music. Some are used to help us navigate our way around and some are used to give instructions along the way.

You will see the **Treble Clef** at the beginning of all guitar music. This tells us where the notes are to be played.

The **Time Signature** is an important sign at the beginning of any piece of music. It tells us how many beats to count in each bar. At a beginners' level it is only really important to look at the **top** number. This will tell you how many beats there are in a bar.

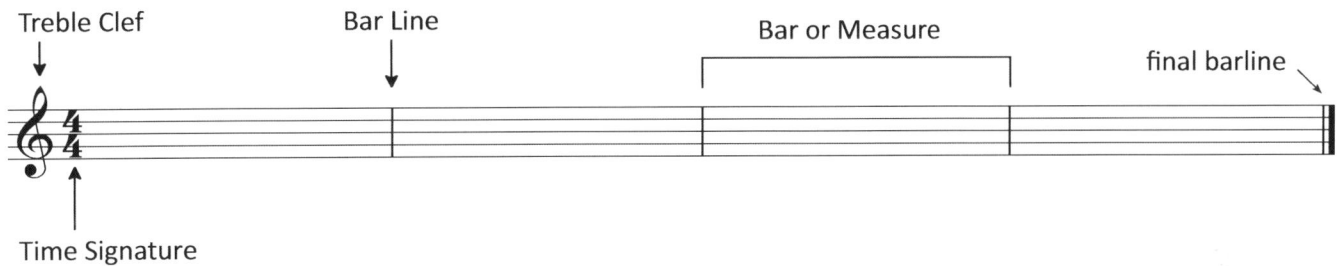

Repeat marks

Sometimes you may want to play the same passage of music more than once. To save writing out that passage of music again we use repeat marks. When you see an end repeat mark you either go back to the opening repeat mark or, if there isn't one, you go back to the beginning of the piece.

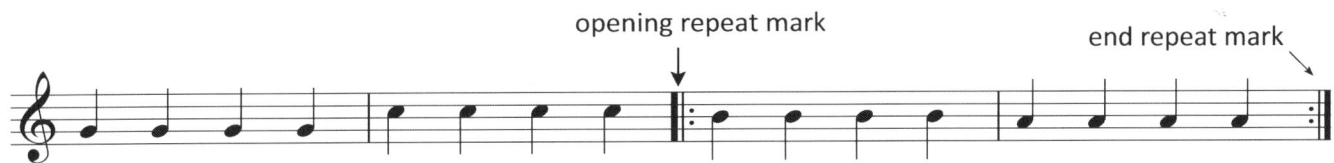

Notes And Note lengths

Some notes last for longer than others. To show these different lengths notes look different according to their duration:

Whole Note
(four beats)

Half Note
(two beats)

Quarter Note
(one beat)

Tablature

Over the years we have developed another helpful way of writing out music for string instruments. This is called **tablature**.

Tablature or **TAB**, as it is commonly known, shows six lines to represent each of the guitar strings. The bottom line is the low **E** string (string 6) and the top line is the top **E** string (string 1). Numbers shown on the TAB stave tell us where to fret notes with the left hand. A '0' (zero) tells us that we are to play the string open. A '2' tells us we need to press that string down at the 2nd fret.

When we have to play chords (two or more notes played at the same time) — they are shown as stacked numbers on the relevant strings.

TAB doesn't tell us the duration of the notes so it is important to read the music stave above so we can play the notes for the correct length of time. The TAB numbers will line up with their corresponding notes in the music stave above making it easier for you to read from left to right.

The open strings of the guitar shown in TAB:

A mixture of open strings & fretted notes:

Single String Exercises

To prepare us for melodies on the guitar we must first get to grips with picking the strings individually. Try the following exercises which will help you to get used to moving between the open strings. Count along as you play. It will help you place the notes correctly in each bar.

Single String Exercise 1

Don't forget to count 4 beats for the whole note

It may help to tap your foot in time with quarter notes. This will help you keep a steady pace for your playing.

In Exercise 2, watch out for the half notes in the 2nd and 4th bars. These last for the last two beats of the bar. Make sure you count their two beats, count beat 3 as you play the note then 4 as the note 'rings on'.

Single String Exercise 2

Half note

Half note

Fretted Notes

Let's try playing a fretted note. The first fretted note you are going to play is **A**. **A** is played on the 2nd fret of the **G** (3rd) string. You should try to use the same number finger of the **left hand** as the fret written. Remember to push down just behind the required fret, not on top of it.

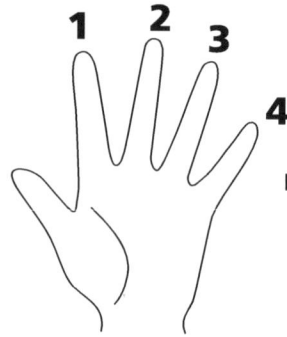

Left hand finger numbers

Fretted Note A

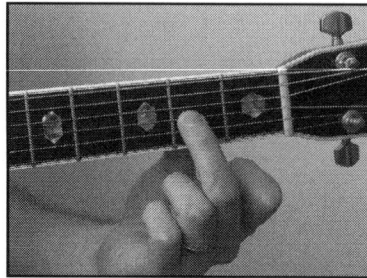

WHAT GOES UP MUST COME DOWN

When you play higher frets (when your left hand moves nearer to your body) you are moving **UP** the guitar neck and when you are playing lower frets you are moving **DOWN** the guitar neck. This often causes confusion with beginners because it is the opposite of what seems logical.

Now try playing the following tune which is made up of a mixture of open strings and your new fretted **A** note. Watch out for the whole note in the last bar and make sure you let it 'ring' for four beats.

New Note A Exercise

Whole note

1   2   3   4

The next new fretted note we are going to learn is **C**. **C** is played on the 1st fret of the **B** (2nd) string — use the 1st or index finger of your left hand.

Fretted Note C

Now try playing the exercises below. They contain your new notes **A** and **C**:

New Notes A & C Exercise 1

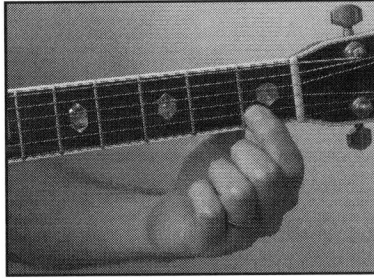

New Notes A & C Exercise 2

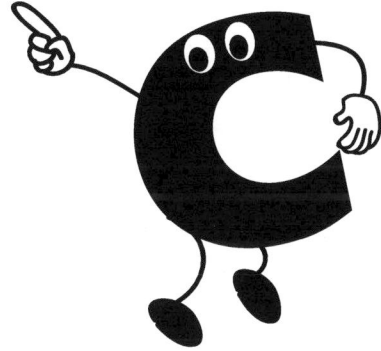

Now let's learn the fretted note **D**. This time it's a 3rd finger note on the 3rd fret of the **B** (2nd) string.

Fretted Note D

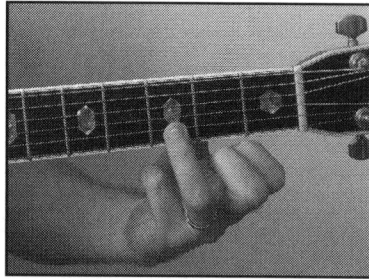

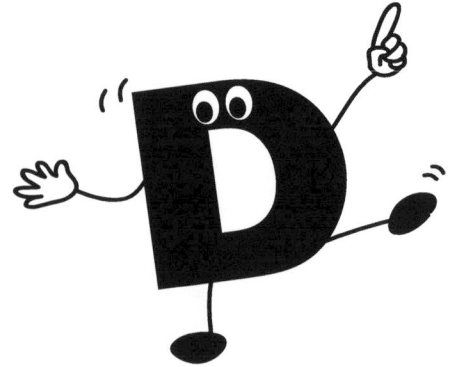

Now we have enough notes to play some simple tunes. Take care when playing to count your two-beat notes.

Mary Had A Little Lamb

Twinkle Twinkle Little Star

Out In The Fields

♪ Scales

The C Major Scale

A scale is a run of notes which go up through a recognized pattern from one note to the same note an **octave** above. An octave is 8 notes ('oct' meaning 8 like 'octopus' or 'octagon'). The note up an octave sounds exactly the same but higher. Try playing your **C** on the **A** string (string 5, fret 3) then play the 1st fret of your **B** string (string 2). Both of these notes are **C**'s but the second is a higher **C**.

Try playing the **C major scale** slowly at first. The C major scale includes some new notes on the lower strings. Make sure you use the correct fingers of your left hand:

Yankee Doodle

The E Minor Pentatonic Scale

The **pentatonic scale** is made up of only 5 notes (hence the 'pent' in it's name, meaning 5). The scale still goes from one note all the way up to its octave above but uses less notes to get there. This scale is the basis of '*The Blues*' and many guitar solos in popular music are built from this simple 5 note scale.

Low Blues

SCALES IN PRACTICE

Scales can be used as a warm-up before practicing. They help strengthen your fingers and are a great way of improving accuracy in fretting. Remember to use the same left hand finger number as the fret you're playing (i.e. finger #1 plays fret #1, finger #2 plays fret #2 and so on).

Flats And Sharps (Accidentals)

From looking at the keyboard of a piano you will see there are white keys and black keys. The black notes are **flats** and **sharps**. These are written as a ♭ symbol for a flat and ♯ symbol for a sharp. These notes also exist on a guitar. They are often referred to as **'Accidentals'**

When you see a **flat** sign before a note it is played one fret **lower** than the natural (normal, un-flattened) version of the note. When you see a **sharp** sign you play the note one fret **higher** than the natural (normal, un-sharpened). Below on the left is your normal fretted note **F** and on the right is your new fretted note **F♯**. Note how the sharpened **F** sits one fret higher than the normal **F** (called a **'natural'**).

Fretted Note F

Fretted Note F♯

Sharps Exercise

Flattening An Open String

Sometimes you may want to flatten an open string. To do this you have to go to the string below to find the new flattened version of your open string note:

 **Open B**

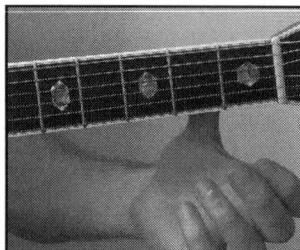

 **Fretted B♭**

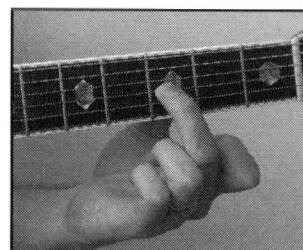

Flat Bread And Beans

KEY SIGNATURES

To save writing out an accidental before every note that needs to be sharpened or flattened we can put the relevant accidentals at the beginning of a piece to tell us to sharpen or flatten those particular notes for the whole piece. This is called a **key signature**. Try playing *'Sharpen Up'* but remember all **F**'s are sharp!

Sharpen Up!

Long Notes And Ties

Long notes such as the whole note and the half note are often harder to play for beginners. This is because you have to count the beats carefully as you wait for your longer notes to ring on.

A **tie** joins two notes together — you only have to play the first note but it now lasts longer (its length + the length of the note it is tied to).

Try playing the following exercise. Remember to count as you go and watch out for the second line when it moves up to half notes.

Playing Long Notes And Ties

Eighth Notes/Quavers

As the pieces you play develop in style and ability you will start to come across **eighth** notes. These last for half a beat. When counting eighth notes use **1 & 2 & 3 & 4 &**. This will help you with the rhythm. Try playing the exercise below.

Frère Jacques

Rests

Rests tell us when not to play. Like notes, they last for different lengths of time. These different lengths are shown as different symbols:

Whole note rest (4 beats or one whole bar)	Half note rest (2 beats)	Quarter note rest (1 beat)	Eighth note rest ($\frac{1}{2}$ beat)

Playing Rests Exercise 1

Playing Rests Exercise 2

Playing Rests Exercise 3

3/4 Or Waltz Time

So far all of our pieces and exercises have been written with 4 beats to a bar. **4/4** is probably the most common time signature you will come across. The other time signature you will see a lot is **3/4** (three beats in a bar). Commonly known as **Waltz** time it was also a popular dance in the late 18th century.

Morning Mood is a tune from composer Edvard Grieg's piece ***Peer Gynt***. Try playing the first quarter note in each bar a little bit louder than the others. This will help you feel the waltz time more effectively. Notice your dotted half notes in this too. These count to three beats so make sure you count them carefully.

Morning Mood

Row, Row

CHORDS

Chords are when you play two or more notes at the same time. Chords are played using 'shapes' which are written using **chord diagrams**.

How To Read Chord Diagrams

These are simple diagrams showing you where to put your left hand fingers. The fingerings are marked just above each box in line with the string below them. The number indicates which of your left hand fingers you should use to push down and fret the note on that string. If the fingering reads '0' then allow that particular string to ring 'open'. When you see an 'X' this means you should try not to play that string as part of your chord.

A

X 0 1 2 3 0 ◄——— LEFT HAND FINGER NUMBERS

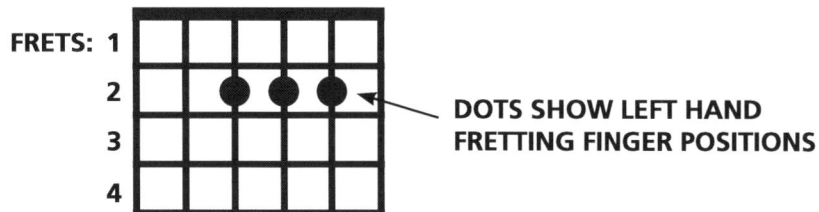

FRETS: 1

2

3

4

DOTS SHOW LEFT HAND
FRETTING FINGER POSITIONS

Strumming

Strumming is when you use your fingers or a pick to brush across all the strings of your chord. Start with your right hand above the strings and swing your hand down across the strings (see below). Most of the movement should come from your wrist but your forearm should swing slightly from the elbow.

Chords: A, D & E

A

X 0 1 2 3 0

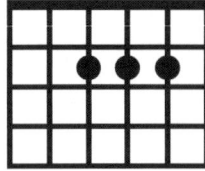

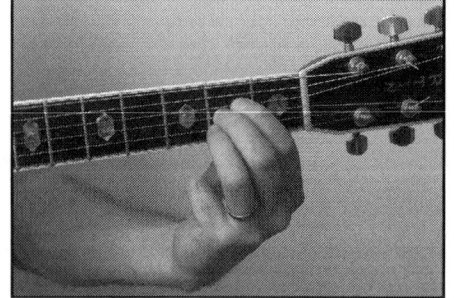

D

X X 0 1 3 2

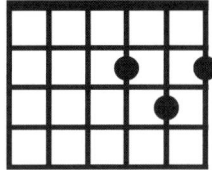

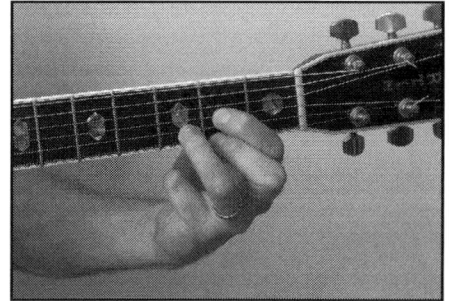

E

0 2 3 1 0 0

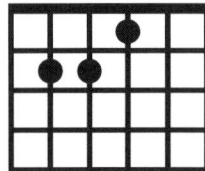

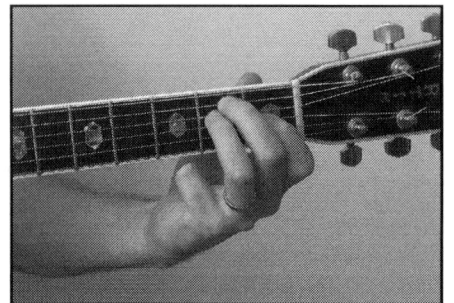

Now try the pattern below. Work towards changing from one chord to another smoothly and quickly. This takes time to master so play the pattern slowly to begin with to give yourself plenty of time to change the chord. Note the repeat bar at the end. This means go back to the beginning and play again.

12-Bar Blues In A

Chords: G, C & D

G

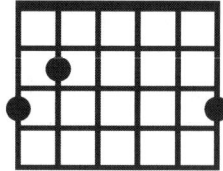

2 1 0 0 0 3

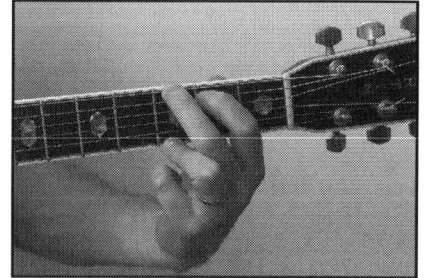

C

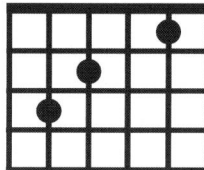

X 3 2 0 1 0

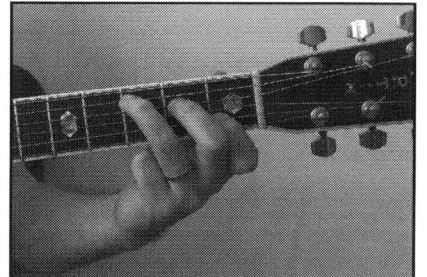

D

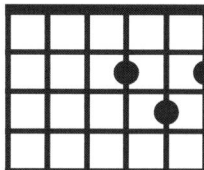

X X 0 1 3 2

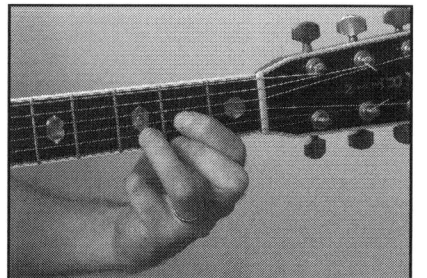

Now try playing the 12-Bar Blues pattern in the key of **G**. Your chords are now **G**, **C** and **D**.
Your new chords **G** and **C** may feel a bit of a stretch but your fingers will soon get used to it!

12-Bar Blues In G

 # Seventh Chords

Seventh chords are very common in guitar music. They make a lovely *'rock & roll'* twangy sound. Next up is your 12-Bar Blues pattern in the key of **A** but this time each chord is a 7th chord.

A7

X 0 2 0 3 0

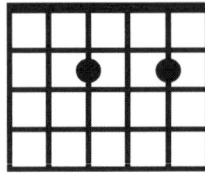

D7

X X 0 2 1 3

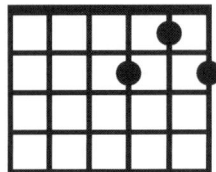

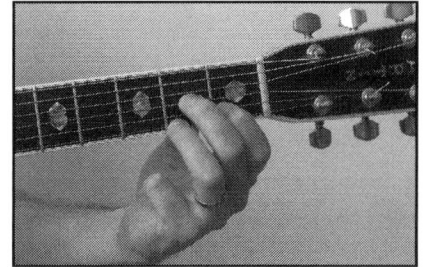

E7

0 2 0 1 0 0

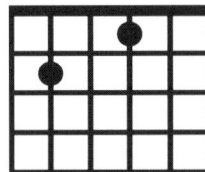

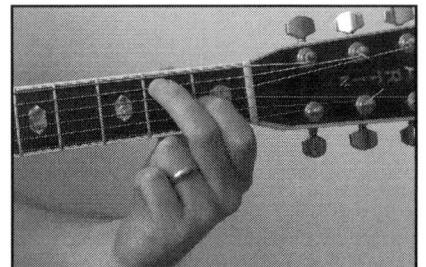

The strumming pattern is slightly different and uses eighth notes towards the end of each bar. Follow the direction arrows to help you with the strumming and try and count *'AND'* on your upstroke.

12-Bar Blues In A With 7ths

Minor Chords

So far we have dealt with **major** chords and **seventh** chords. Now it's time to look at **minor** chords. Where **major** chords sound happy and **seventh** chords sound a little bit more 'bluesy' **minor** chords sound sad. Try playing the **minor** chords below then have a go at strumming through the following two songs.

Am

X 0 2 3 1 0

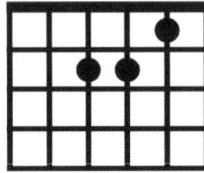

Dm

X X 0 2 3 1

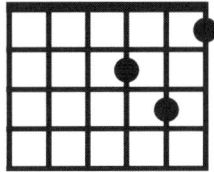

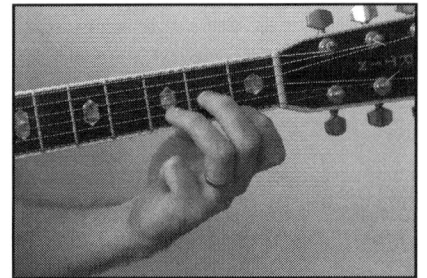

Em

0 1 2 0 0 0

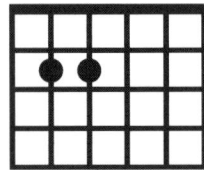

In The Court Of The King

Sad Old Bill

1 & 2 & 3 & 4 & etc.

Fingerpicking

Fingerpicking involves using the thumb and fingers of the right hand to pick out individual notes of the chords. This technique creates an 'arpeggio' where the chord rings on but is broken up into its individual notes. It is important to hold down all fretted notes of the chord until changing to the next chord. The thumb and fingers of the right hand are each given a letter — **p** is the thumb, **i** is the index, **m** is the middle and **a** is the ring finger (or 'anular'). Note this piece is in the key of **G** so all your **F**s will be sharpened.

Rolling Hills

Chord Families

Chords are often used in groups called families. Certain chords work well with other chords and over the years (as with the 12-Bar Blues) very common patterns emerge. Strumming patterns have been given but feel free to try fingerpicking through the patterns too.

Chord Family 1

Chord Family 2

Chord Family 3

More Interesting Strumming Patterns

To give your strumming pattern a bit more 'groove' we can look at 'pushing' some of your strums across beats. The following pattern is an incredibly popular pattern used by players in all genres. It may help you to say the pattern as you're playing it. Try to put a small breath in just after your first '*UP*' (where the tied notes are).

**DOWN DOWN UP,
UP DOWN UP**

Your strumming patterns will develop naturally. The more you play the more you will fall into the most natural way of playing any given rhythm.

Try making up your own strumming pattern using a combination of *UP* strokes and *DOWN* strokes.

Loosen up when strumming but always keep the main beats of the bar clear. Tapping your foot helps.

Higher Notes Further Up The Fretboard

Now lets learn some higher single notes. The exercise below takes you above the 3rd fret of the **E** string right up to the high **A** on the 5th fret. To reach this higher note shift your 1st finger up one fret so it now plays the notes on the 2nd fret. This is known as a **position change**. These are often marked above the music stave using **Roman numerals** and are seen more frequently in classical guitar music.

Higher Notes Excercise

Now try playing *Drunken Sailor* and make sure your left hand shifts position smoothly. The chord boxes for the next few pieces are included and can be played by another player as an accompaniment.

Drunken Sailor

London Bridge Is Falling Down

To play *Treetop Blues* smoothly you have to place your left hand in position 5. This means your 1st finger covers all notes on fret 5 (with finger 2 covering fret 6, finger 3 on fret 7 and finger 4 on fret 8). Note the natural sign ♮ before the **F** in bar 2, 4 & 8. This tells you to play the normal **F** at fret 8 not the sharpened one as shown in the key signature.

Treetop Blues

Riffs

A riff is a repeated pattern of notes, often played on the lower strings of the guitar. Riffs tend to be the memorable or 'catchy' guitar part at the beginning of a song (see Led Zeppelin's *Whole Lotta Love* or The Beatles' *Day Tripper*) they are normally repeated throughout the song.

Riff It Up

CHORD DICTIONARY

Song books for most instruments will include chord names. The following types of chords: Major, Minor and Seventh have all been included in this chord dictionary.

This should enable you to pick up almost any music book and play any of the songs inside. All you have to do is find the chord listed in the following pages, use the fingering shown and play through the song.

Remember when reading chord names you may come across sharp or flat chords not listed in the this chord dictionary. This is because sharps have an equivalent flat which is actually the same note. So:

A♭ is the same as G♯   B♭ is the same as A♯   D♭ is the same as C♯

E♭ is the same as D♯   G♭ is the same as F♯

Try out your own strumming patterns or try fingerpicking through the chords. You will soon find the best approach for the song you're trying to play.

MAJOR CHORDS

A
X 0 1 2 3 0

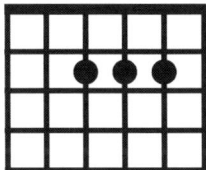

B♭
X X 0 3 4 1

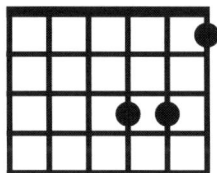

B
X X 2 3 4 1

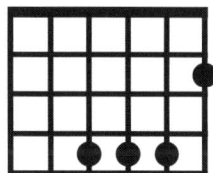

C
X 3 2 0 1 0

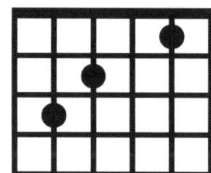

C#
X X 4 1 3 2

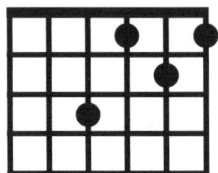

D
X X 0 1 3 2

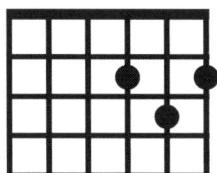

E♭
X X 4 1 3 2

3fr

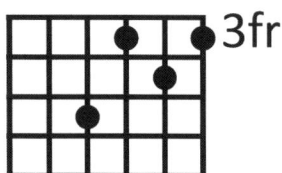

E
0 2 3 1 0 0

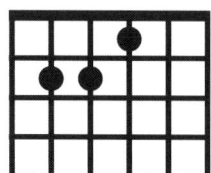

F
X X 4 3 1 2

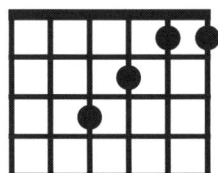

F#
X X 4 3 1 2

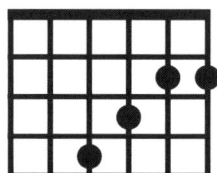

G
2 1 0 0 0 3

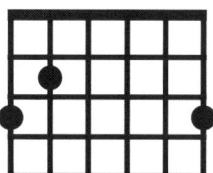

G#
X X 4 3 1 2

4fr

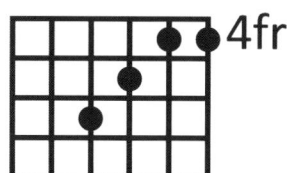

MINOR CHORDS

Am
X 0 2 3 1 0

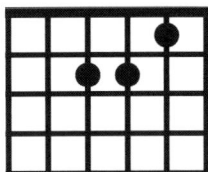

Bbm
X X 3 4 2 1

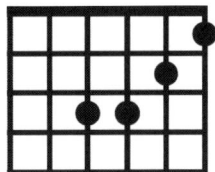

Bm
X X 3 4 2 1

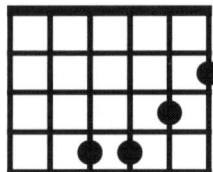

Cm
X X 3 4 2 1

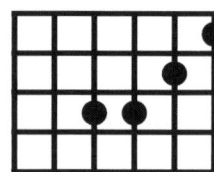 3fr

C#m
X X 2 1 3 0

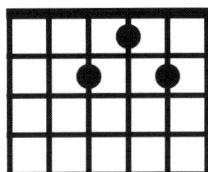

Dm
X X 0 2 3 1

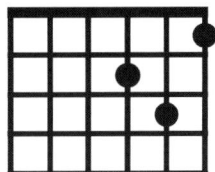

Ebm
X X 3 2 4 1

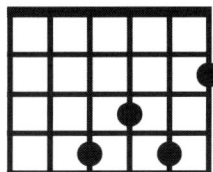

Em
0 1 2 0 0 0

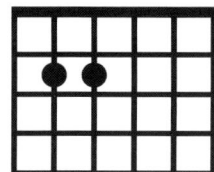

Fm
X X 4 1 2 X

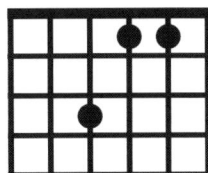

F#m
X X 4 1 2 X

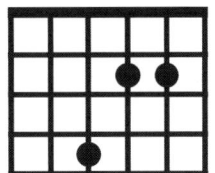

Gm
X X 0 1 2 3

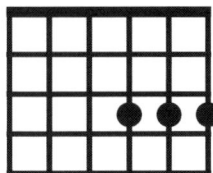

G#m
X X 4 1 2 X

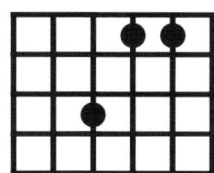 4fr

SEVENTH CHORDS

A⁷
X 0 1 0 3 0

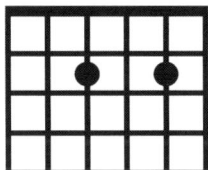

B♭⁷
X X 1 2 3 4
3fr

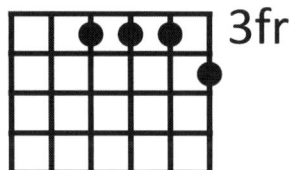

B⁷
X 2 1 3 0 4

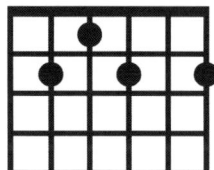

C⁷
X 3 2 4 1 0

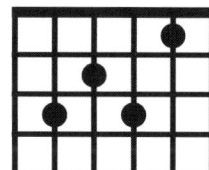

C♯⁷
X 3 2 4 1 X

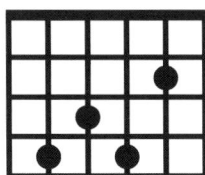

D⁷
X X 0 2 1 3

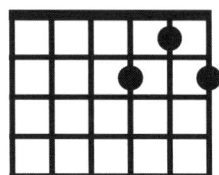

E♭⁷
X X 1 3 2 4

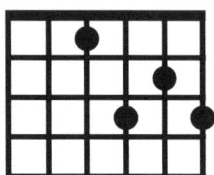

E⁷
0 2 0 1 0 0

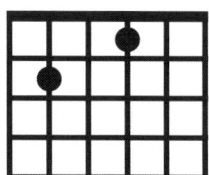

F⁷
X X 1 4 2 3

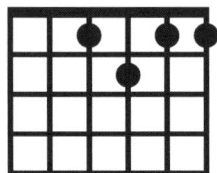

F♯⁷
X X 3 2 1 0

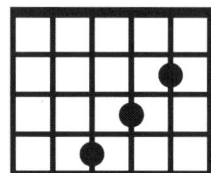

G⁷
3 2 0 0 0 1

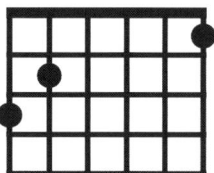

G♯⁷
X X 1 2 3 4

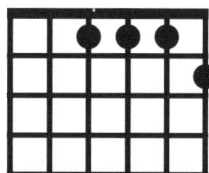

MORE GREAT MUSIC BOOKS FROM KYLE CRAIG!

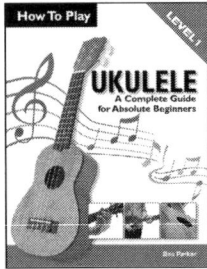

How To Play UKULELE — A Complete Guide for Absolute Beginners

978-1-908-707-08-6

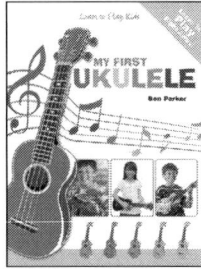

My First UKULELE — Learn to Play: Kids

978-1-908-707-11-6

Easy UKULELE Tunes

978-1-908707-37-6

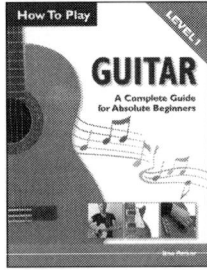

How To Play GUITAR — A Complete Guide for Absolute Beginners

978-1-908-707-09-3

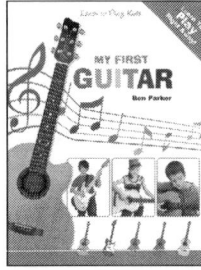

My First GUITAR — Learn to Play: Kids

978-1-908-707-13-0

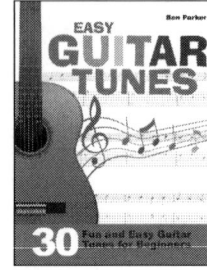

Easy GUITAR Tunes

978-1-908707-34-5

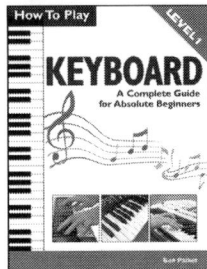

How To Play KEYBOARD — A Complete Guide for Absolute Beginners

978-1-908-707-14-7

My First KEYBOARD — Learn to Play: Kids

978-1-908-707-15-4

Easy KEYBOARD Tunes

978-1-908707-35-2

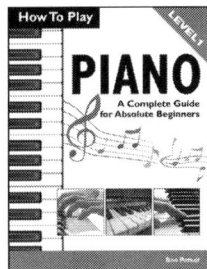

How To Play PIANO — A Complete Guide for Absolute Beginners

978-1-908-707-16-1

My First PIANO — Learn to Play: Kids

978-1-908-707-17-8

Easy PIANO Tunes

978-1-908707-33-8

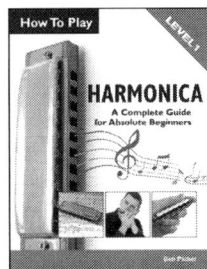

How To Play HARMONICA — A Complete Guide for Absolute Beginners

978-1-908-707-28-4

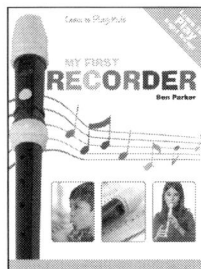

My First RECORDER — Learn to Play: Kids

978-1-908-707-18-5

Easy RECORDER Tunes

978-1-908707-36-9

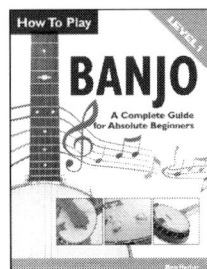

How To Play BANJO — A Complete Guide for Absolute Beginners

978-1-908-707-19-2

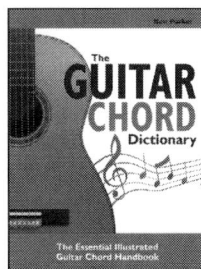

The GUITAR Chord Dictionary

978-1-908707-39-0

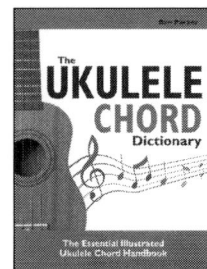

The UKULELE Chord Dictionary

978-1-908707-38-3

Printed in Great Britain
by Amazon